Put Beginning Readers on the Right Track with ALL ABOARD READING™

The All Aboard Reading series is especially designed for beginning readers. Written by noted authors and illustrated in full color, these are books that children really want to read—books to excite their imagination, expand their interests, make them laugh, and support their feelings. With fiction and nonfiction stories that are high interest and curriculum-related, All Aboard Reading books offer something for every young reader. And with four different reading levels, the All Aboard Reading series lets you choose which books are most appropriate for your children and their growing abilities.

Picture Readers
Picture Readers have super-simple texts, with many nouns appearing as rebus pictures. At the end of each book are 24 flash cards—on one side is a rebus picture; on the other side is the written-out word.

Station Stop 1
Station Stop 1 books are best for children who have just begun to read. Simple words and big type make these early reading experiences more comfortable. Picture clues help children to figure out the words. And lots of repetition throughout the text helps children to predict the next word or phrase—an essential step in developing word recognition.

Station Stop 2
Station Stop 2 books are written specifically for children who are reading with help. Short sentences make it easier for early readers to understand what they are reading. Simple plots and simple dialogue help children with reading comprehension.

Station Stop 3
Station Stop 3 books are perfect for children who are reading alone. With longer text and harder words, these books appeal to children who have mastered basic reading skills. More complex stories captivate children who are ready for more challenging books.

In addition to All Aboard Reading books, look for All Aboard Math Readers™ (fiction stories that teach math concepts children are learning in school); All Aboard Science Readers™ (nonfiction books that explore the most fascinating science topics in age-appropriate language); All Aboard Poetry Readers™ (funny, rhyming poems for readers of all levels); and All Aboard Mystery Readers™ (puzzling tales where children piece together evidence with the characters).

All Aboard for happy reading!

To John, the most loyal and die-hard fan I know.

GROSSET & DUNLAP

Published by the Penguin Group
Penguin Group (USA) Inc., 375 Hudson Street, New York, New York 10014, USA
Penguin Group (Canada), 90 Eglinton Avenue East, Suite 700, Toronto, Ontario M4P 2Y3, Canada
(a division of Pearson Penguin Canada Inc.)
Penguin Books Ltd., 80 Strand, London WC2R 0RL, England
Penguin Group Ireland, 25 St. Stephen's Green, Dublin 2, Ireland
(a division of Penguin Books Ltd.)
Penguin Group (Australia), 250 Camberwell Road, Camberwell, Victoria 3124, Australia
(a division of Pearson Australia Group Pty. Ltd.)
Penguin Books India Pvt. Ltd., 11 Community Centre, Panchsheel Park, New Delhi—110 017,
India
Penguin Group (NZ), 67 Apollo Drive, Rosedale, North Shore 0632, New Zealand
(a division of Pearson New Zealand Ltd.)
Penguin Books (South Africa) (Pty.) Ltd., 24 Sturdee Avenue,
Rosebank, Johannesburg 2196, South Africa

Penguin Books Ltd., Registered Offices:
80 Strand, London WC2R 0RL, England

Photo credits: cover/title page: © AP Photo/Frank Gunn; copyright page: © Greg Nelson/Sports Illustrated/
Getty Images; page 5: © Photo by Jesse D. Garrabrant/NBAE via Getty Images; page 7: © AP Photo/J.D.
Pooley; page 13: © AP Photo/Scott R. Galvin; page 15: © Photo by Al Tielemans/Sports Illustrated/Getty
Images; page 16: © Photo by Garrett Ellwood/NBAE via Getty Images; page 18: © Photo by Stephen
Dunn/Getty Images; page 19: © Photo by Michael J. LeBrecht II/Sports Illustrated/Getty Images; page
22: © Photo by Nathaniel S. Butler/NBAE via Getty Images; page 24: © Photo by Rocky Widner/NBAE
via Getty Images; page 27: © Photo by Jesse D. Garrabrant/NBAE via Getty Images; page 29: © AP
Photo/Frank Gunn; page 31: © Photo by Gregory Shamus/NBAE via Getty Images; page 33: © Photo by
Michael J. LeBrecht II/Sports Illustrated/Getty Images; page 35: © Photo by David Dow/NBAE via Getty
Images; page 36: © Photo by Gregory Shamus/Getty Images; page 38: © Photo by Nathaniel S. Butler/
NBAE via Getty Images; page 40: © Photo by David Sherman/NBAE via Getty Images; page 44: ©
(Photo by Bob Rosato /Sports Illustrated/Getty Images; page 46: © AP Photo/Akron Beacon Journal, Phil
Masturzo; page 48: © Photo by Elsa/Getty Images.

Library of Congress Control Number: 2009011513

ISBN 978-0-448-45236-4   10 9 8 7 6 5 4 3 2 1

LEBRON JAMES:
King of the Court

By L.R. Jacobs

With photographs

Grosset & Dunlap

Introduction

LeBron James looked at the shot clock. There were two minutes left in Game 5 of the 2007 Eastern Conference Finals. If his team, the Cleveland Cavaliers, won this game against the Detroit Pistons, they would only be one win away from going to the NBA Finals! The pressure was on!

Only a few minutes ago, the Pistons had been up by seven points. But the Cavaliers were playing great defense. And LeBron had been throwing down fierce dunks. Now, in overtime, the game was tied at 100-98.

But with only 3.1 seconds left in the first overtime, LeBron fouled a Pistons player. The Pistons' player shot two foul shots—and made both! Now they would enter double overtime, the score tied at

100 points. Things did not look good. All the players on the court were exhausted. Yet they pushed through and raced back down the court to the Cavaliers' basket.

With less than three seconds left in double overtime, the Cavaliers knew what to do. They had to get the ball into one man's hands—and that man was LeBron James.

The Cleveland fans were on their

LeBron drives to the hoop in the 2007 NBA Play-offs.

feet cheering. The Detroit fans were screaming, "De-fense, De-fense!" But none of this would distract LeBron. With the shot clock ticking down, LeBron got the ball at midcourt. He started dribbling toward his basket, saw his opening, and leaped up into the air. Even though he was surrounded by the Pistons' defense, LeBron drove in for a layup and, at the last second, scored the game-winning basket! That unbelievable basket gave LeBron a total of 48 points for the game, leading his team to a 109-107 victory! The Cavaliers had won, and LeBron brought his team one step closer to making franchise history by winning an NBA championship.

Growing Up

LeBron James was born on December 30, 1984, in Akron, Ohio. Believe it or not, he shares his birthday with another amazing athlete: Tiger Woods! LeBron's mother, Gloria, was a 16-year-old high school student when LeBron was born. LeBron has never met his father. Although it was difficult raising her son alone, Gloria worked hard to make life as normal as possible for LeBron. Gloria and LeBron

LeBron celebrates with his mom, Gloria.

lived with Gloria's mother, Freda. Gloria's two brothers also helped raise LeBron. LeBron loved being surrounded by his family, but when LeBron was just three years old, Freda passed away. Everyone was very sad.

Without Freda around, Gloria and her brothers had a hard time taking care of LeBron. Neighbors took care of LeBron while Gloria and her brothers worked. Still, the family struggled.

Luckily, LeBron and his mom were able to stay with friends. But each new "home" didn't last long. So, LeBron had to move a lot. This also meant he had to change schools. With each move, he had to make new friends, adjust to new teachers, and catch up on new schoolwork. Yet LeBron was lucky—he had a mother who loved and cared for him.

Even though LeBron's living situation changed a lot, one thing in his life stayed the same. It was his love for sports! LeBron fell in love with basketball at a young age. When he was just three years old, his mother gave him a toy basketball hoop and ball for Christmas. Before Gloria could show him how to shoot the ball, little LeBron taught himself how to slam-dunk! Gloria was amazed.

Besides basketball, LeBron also loved football. In 1994, he joined his first football team, the South Rangers, in Akron's Pee Wee league. In his first season as a wide receiver, he scored 19 touchdowns in six games! He loved learning the rules of the game and making new friends.

One of LeBron's friends on the team was a boy named Frankie Walker Jr. Frankie Jr.'s father, Frankie Sr., was the coach of the team. Frankie Jr. told his father that since LeBron moved around so much, he missed a lot of school. Frankie Sr. didn't want LeBron to fall behind. So he asked Gloria if LeBron could come live with him and his family.

Gloria didn't like the idea of living apart from her son. But she knew it would be good for LeBron to have a steady home. The Walkers would make sure LeBron went to school and kept up with his schoolwork. LeBron was sad to leave his mom, but he knew that they would get to spend the weekends together. So, just before the start of fifth grade, LeBron moved in with the Walker family.

Life in the Walker household was very different for LeBron. He had to do chores around the house, complete his homework every night, and report to school each morning. But all the rules gave LeBron a sense of discipline and routine. He even won the attendance award that year!

But life with the Walkers wasn't all rules and chores. Frankie Sr. coached a youth basketball team, so LeBron and Frankie Jr. joined the team. LeBron worked hard to learn the rules of the game. He quickly became the best player on the team. His coach once said, "LeBron doesn't play golf, but if he picked up some golf clubs, Tiger Woods better watch out." But Frankie Sr. was impressed with much more than LeBron's skill and sportsmanship. He was amazed at how LeBron knew what was going to happen on the court before it even happened. It was as if he was always one step ahead of the rest of the players. LeBron was able to act on his instincts to make the perfect pass, block, or shot.

Frankie Sr. asked LeBron to help him coach the fourth-grade basketball team. LeBron noticed that the younger players looked up to him. They saw him as a role model.

Even though things were going well for LeBron, he really missed his mom. By the time LeBron finished fifth grade, Gloria had found a steady job and gotten an apartment of her own. LeBron got to move back in with his mom!

At age 12, LeBron joined the Amateur Athletic Union (AAU). The AAU is a nation-wide league for top athletes of all sports. The athletes compete against other teams at both the state and national levels (teams from different states across the country).

LeBron became fast friends with three players on his basketball team—Dru Joyce III (also known as Little Dru), Sian Cotton, and

Willie McGee. When they played together on the court, the foursome was unstoppable. Fans even gave them the nickname "The Fab Four." Being on this team also gave LeBron the opportunity to leave Ohio for the first time. His coach said that he cried on one of their first plane rides together! But this time away from home helped LeBron and his new teammates create a strong friendship. LeBron once said, "It was great having those guys around, especially since I didn't have a brother or a sister." LeBron was happy—he was back living with his mom, and had found great friends and great teammates!

LeBron and SVSM seniors huddle up during the last home game of the 2003 season.

The Chosen One

When it came time to go to high school in 1999, LeBron and his new friends wanted to stick together. They all decided to go to the private school St. Vincent-St. Mary (SVSM) in Akron, Ohio. This was a surprising choice. The school was better known for its academic program than for its sports program. But the Fab Four liked SVSM's varsity basketball coach, Coach Dambrot. The boys had practiced with Coach Dambrot at a community center in Akron. They liked his coaching style and they knew they could learn from him.

LeBron stuck out immediately on the basketball team. At six feet, he was much taller than the other players. Plus, he was easily the most talented player on the team.

He led his team to an undefeated season! In the final game of the year, LeBron scored 25 points, grabbed 9 rebounds, passed for 4 assists, and led his team to a championship. Coach Dambrot said, "LeBron would go get 15 points against a bad team, but would make sure everybody else was getting into the game." Right from the beginning, LeBron showed his new coach that he was a

LeBron dunks during the 2003 Prime Time Shootout.

team player who made his teammates play better when they were around him.

The summer after his freshman year of high school, LeBron was invited to attend a Five-Star Basketball training camp in Pittsburgh, Pennsylvania. None of his other friends or teammates were with him at the camp that week.

Even though he would miss playing with the rest of the Fab Four, he knew that this was the time to work hard to improve his overall game. He was so honored to

LeBron and his 2003 teammates pose for the camera.

attend the camp because of all the people who had been there before him. Basketball greats such as Grant Hill, Alonzo Mourning, and LeBron's basketball idol, Michael Jordan, had all attended Five-Star. LeBron looked up to Jordan because he was an amazing, all-around star on the court. Jordan didn't just focus on scoring points or blocking shots. He could do everything, and LeBron wanted to be just like him.

When LeBron returned to school for his sophomore year, all of his hard work at training camp began to pay off. He had the best sophomore season of any student in Ohio, scoring an average of more than 20 points and receiving more than 7 rebounds per game. LeBron led his team to a Division-III championship for the second year in a row. His fans started calling him "King James." More and more

fans wanted the chance to see this high school player in action. LeBron's school had to move the games to a larger arena to hold everyone! But the most important person in that huge arena was always LeBron's mom. She came to the games wearing a jersey that said "LeBron's Mom" on the back.

Throughout the next three years in high school, LeBron won many awards. He was named Ohio's Mr. Basketball in 2001, 2002, and 2003. This was an award only for high school students. He appeared on the cover of *Sports Illustrated* magazine in 2002. The magazine called him "The

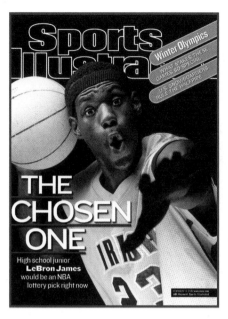

Chosen One" of high school basketball. It was a big honor. He was seen as the future of the National Basketball Association (NBA), a place once held by Michael Jordan. Rumors started to spread that LeBron would be the number one draft pick for the NBA after only his third year in high school. The NBA rarely takes athletes straight out of high school! Nike and Adidas, two major shoe companies, each offered LeBron a lot of money to wear their shoes.

Despite all the attention, LeBron kept working hard in his classes. He wanted to get good grades. He knew it was important to finish high school before moving on to professional sports. Lots of magazine and newspaper articles were written about LeBron. But people quickly realized that LeBron was just like any other normal kid. He did his homework and hung out with his friends after school when he wasn't playing hoops.

In April 2003, at the end of his four years in high school, LeBron announced that he would enter the NBA Draft, instead of playing college basketball. LeBron and his mom both knew this would help them financially. Plus, it would be an opportunity to fulfill Lebron's dream of playing professional basketball. This was big news for the sports world. Everyone wanted to know two things: Which team would LeBron James join? And would an 18-year-old, high school star be able to go up against the older and more experienced pros in the NBA?

The Real Deal

When it was time for the 2003 NBA Draft, there was no question who the number one pick would be—LeBron James! LeBron had showed everyone that he was the best high school basketball player in the country. The media said he was even better than the older and more experienced college players that year in the draft. But which team would have the number one pick this year?

For the draft lottery, each team is given a certain amount of tickets based on how they did during the previous season. The team with the worst record gets the most tickets, so that team has the best chance of getting the number one pick. For the 2002-2003 season, the Cleveland Cavaliers got the number one pick in the lottery.

On June 23, to no one's surprise, the Cavaliers picked LeBron James. LeBron was excited to stay in Ohio. This meant he would be close to all of his teammates, friends, and coaches from high school, and, most importantly, his mom.

Once LeBron signed with the

LeBron and the other 2003 draft picks get ready to join the NBA.

Cavaliers, he followed in the footsteps of his idol Michael Jordan, and accepted an offer from Nike. Nike paid LeBron millions of dollars to wear its clothes and endorse its products. LeBron was probably very happy with all that money, and he knew just what to do with it—spend it on his mom. After all the years Gloria spent struggling to support her son, he could finally repay her! It was a great moment for LeBron.

LeBron's NBA debut game took place on October 29, 2003, against the Sacramento Kings. Everyone was excited to see how this kid straight out of high school would play against NBA athletes. People wondered if the pressure would be too much for him. But LeBron came through for his fans. He played one of the best games any rookie has ever played. He

LeBron James marks his entrance to the NBA with a slam dunk.

scored 25 points! In the last few minutes of the game, he stole the ball, raced down the court, and scored with a massive slam dunk! A minute later, he stole the ball again. Everyone expected him to show off with another dunk, but instead, LeBron did something completely unexpected. He passed the ball to Ricky Davis, who scored the basket instead. Now, that's being a team player!

That night, LeBron James scored more points than Michael Jordan did in his debut game in the NBA! (Michael Jordan scored 16 points.) LeBron was just as good as everyone thought he was. And he had proved he was a true team player who could ensure a win for his team. He was "the real deal," as one Sacramento Kings player called him.

Even though LeBron helped the Cavaliers win many games that season, the team had a record of 35-47. Still, they won more games in that season than in the year before, when they only won 17 games. Ticket sales soared and LeBron's jersey, number 23, quickly became the fastest-selling jersey in the league. LeBron must have felt great to bring such excitement to the Cavs, and to the NBA.

Fans packed the stadium night after night to watch LeBron play. People were amazed by his size at 6'8". And they were wowed by his speed and ability to move around anyone who tried to block him. He made it almost impossible for other players to guard him. The San Antonio Spurs coach once said, "If he gets his shoulders square near the basket and you don't get a hand on him, he's impossible to stop."

LeBron won the 2004 Rookie of the Year award. At 18 years old, he was the youngest player to ever receive this award. Nobody was surprised. LeBron finished the season with an average of 20.9 points, 5.5 rebounds, and 1.6 steals per game. When he accepted the award, he thanked his coaches and teammates, and, of course, he thanked his mom. "She has been there since day one . . ." he said as he thanked Gloria.

During the summer between his first and second years in the NBA, LeBron was asked to play on Team USA in the 2004 Summer Olympics in Athens, Greece. It was a huge honor. He was able to play alongside some of the greats he had always admired: Tim Duncan, Carmelo Anthony, and Allen Iverson. Even though Team USA didn't win the gold that summer, LeBron still managed to bring home a bronze medal. He would later help Team USA win the gold medal in the 2008 Beijing Olympics.

LeBron shows off his olympic gold medal with Team USA teammates Kobe Bryant and Chris Paul.

Road to the Finals

LeBron had a rocky start to his sophomore year in the NBA. But one of LeBron's best games in the 2004-2005 season was against the Toronto Raptors on March 20, 2005. As the teams played into the fourth quarter, LeBron was approaching 40 points, with no sign of slowing down. With 12 minutes left in the game, the crowd began to wonder if he could score 50 points. LeBron continued to score. With just over two minutes left to play, he finally broke the 50-point mark! He had a huge grin on his face as he sunk that last shot, but he kept his head in the game. The Cavaliers didn't beat the Raptors. But that night LeBron became the youngest player in the NBA to score more than 50 points in one game. He ended up scoring

56 points. This was only the first of many "youngest player" records LeBron would blast through.

LeBron had achieved a lot during

The Raptors defense can't stop LeBron from scoring.

his first two years in the NBA. Still, he wanted to help his team improve and win even more games in the 2005-2006 season. The Cavaliers played its first game of that season against the New Orleans Hornets on November 2. Every fan in the stadium, including the Hornets fans, had come to see "King James" hold court, and they were not disappointed.

With just a few minutes left in the second quarter, LeBron made four three-pointers in a row! The Hornets tried to break up his shooting streak with a time-out. It didn't work. LeBron came out of the time-out even more fired up and ready to play! He scored several more baskets that night. At one point, he even blew on his fingertips to signal that they were on fire! Both the fans and the other players were in awe that night. "We were just like the fans. We wanted him to keep shooting!" said teammate Donyell Marshal. The Cavs won the game, 109-87.

After that game, the team went on a hot streak, winning eight straight games. In the November 13 game against the Orlando Magic, LeBron became the youngest player to score 4,000 points in his career. LeBron was probably very happy to set another

LeBron attempts a three-pointer against the Hornets.

"youngest player" record, but knew he couldn't get caught up in his success. He wanted his team to make it to the play-offs. That wish came true when the Cavaliers ended the season with a record of 50-32. The Cavs were in the play-offs!

The top eight teams from each conference (there are two: the Eastern and Western Conferences) make it to the play-offs. The first round determines who will go to the Eastern and Western Conference Semifinals. The winners of those series then go on to the next round, the conference finals. Then the Eastern and Western Conference Champions go up against each another in the NBA Finals. The winner of that game wins the NBA Championship.

The Cavaliers made it through the first round. They defeated the Washington Wizards four games to two in a best-of-seven series. Next stop was the Eastern Conference Semifinals against the Detroit Pistons, a team known for its excellent defense. As good as LeBron was, it wasn't enough. The Pistons put two and sometimes three of their players on LeBron at once; this is called double- and triple-teaming. LeBron was frustrated. The Cavaliers lost the series four games to three. The road to that year's NBA Finals ended there for LeBron and his teammates.

The Cavs huddle up during a time-out.

LeBron returned the next season still determined to help his team improve their record. He broke more "youngest player" records. One sportswriter even joked, "James may have to legally change his name to 'LeBron James, the youngest player ever' as it seems he hits these milestones on a regular basis." But LeBron didn't focus on these individual achievements. He focused on his team. They finished their season with a 50-32 record, and LeBron finished that season averaging 27.3 points, 6.7 rebounds, and 6 assists per game.

The Cavaliers beat the Washington Wizards and the New Jersey Nets in the first two rounds of the play-offs. Next, they had to play for the Eastern Conference Championship. Once again, they faced the Detroit Pistons. LeBron was determined to beat them this time. And they did it. The Cavs wrapped up the series in six games. After the series, LeBron told reporters, "This is probably the best feeling I've ever had in my life." But LeBron couldn't rest. The Cavs still had to face the Western Conference Champions, the San Antonio Spurs, in the NBA Finals.

The Cavaliers played hard. But it

LeBron shows off the 2007 Eastern Conference trophy.

wasn't enough to beat the Spurs. San Antonio swept the Cavaliers and won the NBA Championship. Yet for LeBron and his team, getting to the NBA Finals was a huge accomplishment. This was the farthest they had come since LeBron joined the team. He had taken his team from last place to second place in a few short years. However,

fans wondered if the Cavaliers would *ever* be good enough to win a championship.

Just as the Cavs were getting into a groove of winning games, the team faced a big challenge.

An injured LeBron watches from the bench.

During one of their first games of the 2007-2008 season, LeBron sprained his left finger as he went up for a shot. He had to sit out for several games. LeBron hated watching from the bench. He wanted to be on the court, helping his team win games. This was the first time the Cavs had played without LeBron since he joined the team. The team felt his absence on the court. They lost all five games played without him.

But LeBron turned things around the minute he stepped back on the court. The Cavaliers won 11 out of 14 games in the month of January. With LeBron's help, the team turned their record around from 14-17 to 25-20. They would make it to the play-offs for the third year in a row.

The Cavaliers made it through the first round. Then they had to face one of the best teams in the NBA—the Boston Celtics, led by NBA great Kevin Garnett—in the Eastern Conference Semifinals. The Celtics had a 66-16 record that year! Going into game 7, the teams were tied at three games each. That game would decide who would move on to the NBA Finals.

There was only 2:20 left of the game and the Celtics were winning with a score of 89-86. Boston had the ball. LeBron kept a close guard on Paul Pierce, Boston's leading scorer for the night. Lebron saw an opening

Garnett tries to guard King James in the 2007 Eastern Conference Semifinals.

and stole the ball! He raced down the court. He slammed the ball through the net to bring the game within one point. But the Celtics went on to win both the game (97-92) and the series. Once again, the Cavaliers would go home empty-handed. But LeBron didn't give up. Instead, he concentrated on working hard in the off-season. He had to be ready for the 2008-2009 season.

When LeBron returned for his sixth season, he knew he would face challenging players. But LeBron still had a lot going for him. His size, speed, strength, and great athletic ability make it very hard for people to guard him. Unlike Shaquille O'Neal, who stands at 7'1", LeBron can change directions even when he's already in the air! He's able to shift and twist to the left or right within seconds to avoid being blocked by an opponent. And once he's up in the air, there

LeBron dunks in a game againt the Minnesota Timberwolves in 2007.

is no stopping the strength and force of that dunk as it comes crashing through the net.

LeBron set a new career record by playing 81 games in the regular season. He pushed himself harder than he ever had: He was on a mission. His hard-working season paid off. King James was given a new crown: the Most Valuable Player (MVP) award for the 2008-2009 season. He finished the season with a per game average of 28.4 points, 7.6 rebounds, and 7.2 assists.

LeBron helped his team finish with a 66-16 record, which won them the top seed in the play-offs—a first for the Cavaliers! When he accepted his award, he thanked his teammates. "Individual accolades come when team success happens," he said. It must have felt great for LeBron to be able to accept that award in the place where his rise to fame began: St. Vincent-St. Mary's gymnasium.

LeBron helped his team sweep the Detroit Pistons in four games in the first round of the play-offs. LeBron and his teammates must have been feeling great as they went into the second round of the play-offs against the Atlanta Hawks. They must have felt even better when they swept that series in four straight games, too! But LeBron knew he couldn't rest yet. "My mission hasn't been completed," he told reporters. LeBron and his teammates still had a lot of work to do.

The Cavaliers faced the Orlando Magic in the Eastern Conference Finals. Their star player, Dwight Howard, won the Defensive Player of the Year award that season. The Magic watched the Cavaliers' opponents lose in four straight games because they couldn't guard LeBron. Dwight Howard made sure his team was ready for the NBA MVP. The Magic won Game 1 107-106. Still, LeBron had a great game. He scored a career high of 49 points. He made 20 of 30 shots for the night, had 6 rebounds, 8 assists, 2 steals, and 3 blocks. LeBron must have been frustrated that his team didn't win. But he held onto a positive attitude. "Series are not won or lost in one game. We have to make some adjustments," he told reporters after the game.

With the Magic ahead by one game, the Cavaliers returned for Game 2 ready to win. In the last seconds of the game, LeBron proved to everyone why he was crowned MVP. The Cavaliers were down by two points. LeBron got the ball with less than a second on the clock. He put up one of his usual off balance, twisting shots that rattled through the rim! The Cavaliers won 96-95. The series was now tied at one game each. Next, the Cavaliers headed down to Orlando for Games 3 and 4. The Magic won Game 3, 99-89, giving them a 2-1 lead in the series. Then the Magic won Game 4 116-114. The Cavaliers were headed back to Cleveland down three games to one in the series. If the Magic won Game 5, the Cavaliers would be out. Luckily, the Cavaliers were able to hold on for one more game, winning Game 5 112-102. LeBron's outstanding performance in the fourth quarter kept the team alive that night: He scored or assisted on 32 consecutive points.

The Cavaliers went back to Orlando for Game 6. They needed to win this game to tie the series at three a piece. But in the end, the Magic won the game 103-90, send-

ing the Cavaliers home. Many people thought the Cavs would come out on top of the 2008-2009 season. But they were wrong. Cleveland fans and LeBron would have to wait until next season for a chance at the championship.

LeBron drives to the hole against the Magic.

Up Close and Personal

Despite LeBron's amazing achievements on the court, he has never let his fame affect who he is. LeBron never takes all the credit for a Cavaliers win, no matter how many points he has scored. He sees himself as part of the team. He once said, "Individual aspects mean nothing to me. I'm a team player. I just want to see our team winning games." And this has gotten him respect from his teammates and coaches. Even though he could score more than 50 points in a game, LeBron never acts like he is better than anyone else on the team. When he first joined the Cavaliers, LeBron carried balls to the team bus before games as part of a Cavaliers ritual for new guys.

LeBron has broken many NBA records since joining the Cavs. Yet, he always

remembers that there is more to life than basketball. There is nothing more important to him than his family. His mom comes to all of his home games. She still wears that jersey that says "LeBron's Mom!" He likes that he has been able to stay in Ohio, close to his family and community.

LeBron has never forgotten the hard times he and his mother went through when he was growing up. He is probably very happy that he is successful now, but he wants to give back to his community. He wants to help others who are in need. LeBron started his own charity, the James Family Foundation, that helps single-parent families. One of the biggest events they have is the King for Kids bike-a-thon. LeBron always participates to raise as much money as possible. He is also involved in the NBA's Read to Achieve program, for which he visits classrooms to read aloud to students. And at the start of every school year, LeBron donates backpacks filled with school supplies.

LeBron has told reporters that he just wants to be a regular guy who helps make the world a better place. LeBron works hard and is dedicated to his team. He is also devoted to helping kids and people in need, and has become a role model. It's only a matter of time before he helps the Cleveland Cavaliers win an NBA Championship.